March 10th — Friday — Hawkwell

Bus Stop

A Comedy

Rae Shirley

Sunday 5th March
Rehearsal — Scout Hut
2 pm.

11 Feb — Quiz Night, Hawkwell 7.30 for 8

Heather's House
46 Bull Lane

Wendy
146 A Swan Lane
Tel. 01268 734308

Samuel French — London
New York — Sydney — Toronto — Hollywood

> Basic fee for each and every
> performance by amateurs   Code C
> in the British Isles

ISBN 0 573 13209 7

MADE AND PRINTED IN GREAT BRITAIN BY
LATIMER TREND & COMPANY LTD PLYMOUTH

MADE IN ENGLAND

Please note our NEW ADDRESS:

Samuel French Ltd
52 Fitzroy Street London W1P 6JR
Tel: 01 - 387 9373

PRODUCTION NOTES

This play is written primarily for seven women. If it is possible to include a man in the cast the dialogue between **page 9 and ** page 10 may be included. Otherwise simply cut this dialogue. The two lovers are only walk-on parts and the female half may be doubled by the BOOKWORM. If you have difficulty in finding even seven women, let alone a man, the BOOKWORM may be played by either ANITA or FIONA as there is ample time to change costumes.

WOMAN I	knows her own mind and makes sure that everybody else knows it as well. She wears a hat back to front and is determinedly fractious. She should be middle-aged and obviously has ruled her husband with a rod of iron for many years.
WOMAN II	is rather a simple soul, a middle-aged romantic and a complete contrast to WOMAN I. She is obviously embarrassed by the other's brashness but, for the most part, sticks by her just the same.
MRS HICKERY	doesn't think too much of WOMAN I and II. She is also middle-aged and all for a bit of gossip - generally good natured. Apart from her bags of shopping and an umbrella she carries a bag of chips wrapped up in newspaper.
MRS FINNEY	is a friend of MRS HICKERY and her soul-mate in gossip. She's a bit more basic than MRS HICKERY but doesn't like to be downright rude - unlike WOMAN I.
ALL FOUR WOMEN	are weighed down with shopping bags of all sizes and descriptions.
ANITA & FIONA	are two well-dressed and obviously well-heeled women. They speak rather over-done queen's English and you should feel they're about to name drop any second. They are both very smart and are sporting lush-looking handbags - obviously they wouldn't be seen dead with anything as low and common as a shopping bag - although ANITA may have a dainty decorative openwork type of basket in which resides a solitary small package. FIONA is wearing a fur coat (something that will pass as mink). ANITA must be middle-aged as

she can remember the last war ('39-'45) but
FIONA can be younger.

The BOOKWORM   is wearing granny specs at the end of her nose
                 and is vaguely donnish. She has a bright coloured
                 beret stuck on the back of her head and a shoulder
                 bag draped carelessly over one shoulder. She is
                 engrossed in a large tome - perhaps one on middle
                 English studies. She can be any age from mid-
                 twenties upwards.

The LOVERS   are much too wrapped up in themselves to warrant
                 a description so they remain up to the producer
                 who may include or exclude them as she decides.

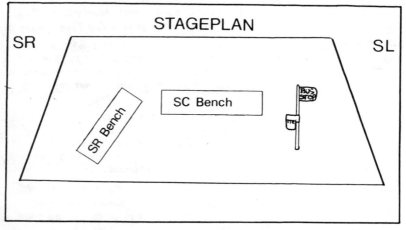

STAGEPLAN

SR   SL

SR Bench   SC Bench

W II begins sitting on short bench (right hand side).

BUS STOP

Set: A bus stop in any small provincial town. There are two benches on stage, one SC facing audience, the other at a slight angle to it SR. SL is the bus stop sign; attached to it is a litter bin. The bottom of the bin is missing, though this should not be discernible to the audience.

The curtain rises on WOMAN I seated on the SC bench, looking as if she's been there since time immemorial. On the bench each side of her are planted bulging shopping bags and there is another at her feet.

There is a slight pause while the audience takes in the scene. Then she looks impatiently at her watch, gets up, nearly trips over the bag at her feet, mutters an unladylike expletive and taking a few steps L peers into the wings, obviously hoping against hope that she will see a bus - she doesn't..... She sits down again, rummages in one of the shopping bags, fishes out a brown paper bag, takes out a banana and with her little finger at a dainty angle munches away. She demolishes about half, then carefully folds the skin over the remaining portion and returns it to the bag. WOMAN II enters SL after this performance. She is also carrying bags of shopping.

WOMAN II	Morning. You waiting for the bus?
WOMAN I	What d'you reckon I'm doing? Having a sauna?
WOMAN II	(bemused) Having a what?
WOMAN I	Never mind! Yeh, I'm waiting for a bus all right. Been here this past half-hour and no sign of it yet.
WOMAN II	(cheerfully) Oh, never say die, I say. P'rhaps he's having a cuppa tea.
WOMAN I	'Oo?
WOMAN II	The bus driver. It's thirsty work, driving a bus.
WOMAN I	It's thirsty work waiting for one, an' all.

enter S.L — (to WOMAN I line)

left hand side.
(WOMAN II sits on same bench as WOMAN I and starts disposing of her bags.)

WOMAN II	Might as well take the weight off my legs, I suppose.
WOMAN I	You'll be daft if you don't. I never stand when I gets a chance to sit.
WOMAN II	You got trouble with your legs?
WOMAN I	Varicose veins, that's what I got.
WOMAN II	You never!
WOMAN I	A regular scenic railway.
WOMAN II	Fancy!
WOMAN I	All the way up to me 'ips, they are.
WOMAN II	As far as that?
WOMAN I	That's right.
WOMAN II	I never 'eard of them as far as that.
WOMAN I	Well, you 'ave now.
WOMAN II	That's right. I have, haven't I?
WOMAN I	Doctor said he never seen anything like it.
WOMAN II	Fancy!
WOMAN I	Wanted to make me a special case.
WOMAN II	What d'you mean - special case?
WOMAN I	Well, you know - go into hospital and have a lot of them doctors go over you.
WOMAN II	Go over you? Oh, I wouldn't like that, no, indeed I wouldn't! Did y'go?
WOMAN I	Not me. Didn't fancy it.
WOMAN II	I don't blame you.
WOMAN I	(with a sniff) My 'usband did.
WOMAN II	You mean - your husband fancied it?
WOMAN I	No! Blamed me for not going. He said to me - don't you come grumbling to me again when you had the chance to have all your veins out.
WOMAN II	Oh dear!
WOMAN I	Very cold man, my husband.

WOMAN II	Oh, my husband wouldn't have pushed me into anything like that.
WOMAN I	Oh? Why not?
WOMAN II	(confidentially) To tell you the truth.... (looks around as if the pavement had ears) ... to tell you the truth - I'm a very shy girl.
WOMAN I	(seeing her in a new light) Is that a fact?
WOMAN II	(nodding) It is.
WOMAN I	What exactly d'you mean - shy girl?
WOMAN II	(bashfully) Well, you know ..... modest.
WOMAN I	Modest?
WOMAN II	That's right. My husband calls me 'Modesty Mabel'.
WOMAN I	Modesty Mabel! Well, I be .....
WOMAN II	I even undresses in the dark.
WOMAN I	In the dark? My gawd! Whatever for?
WOMAN II	(eyes lowered) Well, me husband's there, you see.
WOMAN I	Well, he would be, wouldn't he?
WOMAN II	And I like to keep up the delusion.
WOMAN I	Delusion? What d'you mean - delusion?
WOMAN II	The romantic delusion, o'course.
WOMAN I	(dead serious) Oh, that one.
WOMAN II	I believes in a woman keeping a bit of mystery about her.
WOMAN I	Well, if you keep on undressing in the dark it would be a mystery, wouldn't it?
WOMAN II	That's right, dear. That's why I do it.
WOMAN I	We had to undress in the dark last winter, me and my 'usband.
WOMAN II	Oh! Feeling romantic, were you?
WOMAN I	Romantic - with me 'usband! You got to be joking?

WOMAN II	What then?
WOMAN I	Power cut.
WOMAN II	Oh, that.
WOMAN I	Me 'usband cracked his toe against the bed and I went flying over the what-d'you-call-it.
WOMAN II	Oh dear!
WOMAN I	Didn't do me varicose veins any good, I can tell you.
WOMAN II	Well, it wouldn't, would it?
WOMAN I	Ended up with me sleeping on me own in the best bedroom. Frozen stiff I were.
WOMAN II	Very cold winter, last winter.
WOMAN I	And him snoring away in the back bedroom fit to wake the dead. Only does it to annoy me.
WOMAN II	Oh dear.
WOMAN I	If you were married to him, he'd soon put paid to your romantic delusions, I can tell you.
WOMAN II	Oh dear!
WOMAN I	Had five bursts that self-same night.
WOMAN II	Oh dear!
WOMAN I	Three in the bathroom and two in the you-know-what.
WOMAN II	Oh dear!
WOMAN I	Talk about row for the shore, boys!
WOMAN II	Water everywhere, was there?
WOMAN I	I said to my 'usband, 'you'd better get the fire brigade', I said. And you know what he went and said?
WOMAN II	Not yet I don't.
WOMAN I	Well, I won't repeat the language, seeing as we're both ladies - and you so modest an'all....
WOMAN II	That's right.
WOMAN I	'Fire brigade be -ahem- ,' he said, 'what we

want is a lifeboat and a raft!'

WOMAN II	Oh dear.
WOMAN I	No sense of humour, that's his trouble.
WOMAN II	If there's one thing my husband's got, it's a sense of humour.
WOMAN I	Oh?
WOMAN II	Always laughing, he is. Mind you, there's times I wish I knew what he was laughing at.
WOMAN I	You mean you don't know?
WOMAN II	No .... not half the time, I don't. On a Monday morning when he rolls out of bed and it's pouring cats and dogs for washing day, laughing fit to bust he is.
WOMAN I	Sounds a bit - well, never mind!
WOMAN II	Tell me, Bert, I says to him - that's his name, Bert - what you laughing at, darling? I always calls him darling.
WOMAN I	Keeping up the romantic delusion?
WOMAN II	That's right. But he never tells me - just keeps on laughing. Dead funny, that.
WOMAN I	You can say that again!
WOMAN II	Sometimes I join in - just to show willing, like - but I don't know what I'm laughing at.
WOMAN I	(drily) There's nowt as queer as folk.
WOMAN II	Pardon?
WOMAN I	Old proverb. Scotch I think, or Irish or something.
	(MRS HICKERY enters SL heavily laden and carrying a bag of chips wrapped up in newspaper.)
MRS HICKERY	Bus not gone yet?
WOMAN I	(true to form) Well, if it had, we wouldn't be here, would we?
MRS HICKERY	You could have just missed it, couldn't you?
WOMAN I	We could have, but we didn't.

WOMAN II	(in an effort to spread sweetness and light) Should be here any minute now.
WOMAN I	You hope!
WOMAN II	Well, I've been here at least ten minutes, so –
WOMAN I	Ten minutes! I've been here more than half an hour and I haven't so much as smelt one yet!
WOMAN II	Yes, well, come to think of it, you were here before me, weren't you?
WOMAN I	That's what I'm saying.
MRS HICKERY	Look, I don't care if the pair of you have been here since Christmas – so you can stop arguing.
WOMAN I	(belligerently) Who's arguing?
WOMAN II	(appeasingly) Nice morning, ain't it?
MRS HICKERY	It said rain on the telly. That's why I brought my umbrella.
WOMAN I	Always wrong, they are. I'd rather trust my corns.
MRS HICKERY	Well, all I hope is that the bus won't be too long. I got some chips here for my dinner.
WOMAN II	Thought I could smell something nice.
MRS HICKERY	I made them put some extra paper round them so they'd keep nice and hot.
WOMAN I	No fish?
MRS HICKERY	What d'you mean – no fish?
WOMAN I	Didn't you get some fish?
MRS HICKERY	Not me.
WOMAN II	Don't you like fish?
MRS HICKERY	(I like it all right. It don't like me.) No
WOMAN II	Fancy!
MRS HICKERY	(Plays merry hell with my stomach.) I only got to see a tin of sardines and I start to 'eave.
WOMAN II	Oh dear!
MRS HICKERY	I'll fry an egg with 'em when I get home. Egg

and chips and a bit of fresh bread and butter,
~~with a cuppa tea.~~ Nice as anything.

WOMAN I   I like a nice bit of gammon myself.

MRS HICKERY   (drily) Don't we all!) 1/ Like bacon better!

WOMAN I   Grilled, o'course.

WOMAN II   Fancy that - grilled!

WOMAN I   If I had my way, I'd chuck every frying-pan into
                       the bottom of the sea.

WOMAN II   Never!

WOMAN I   I would. Plays havoc with your insides, frying-
                       pans do.

WOMAN II   Oh, I don't know. I like frying-pans.

WOMAN I   You got ulcers yet?

WOMAN II   (protestingly) I haven't even got a pimple!

WOMAN I   You wait!

WOMAN II   And I'm always frying things.

MRS HICKERY   Me, too. I even fry beans in tomato sauce.

WOMAN II   I'll have to try that. O-oh, those chips do
                       smell nice.

WOMAN I   The pair of you haven't started frying soup yet,
                       have you?

WOMAN II   (seriously) I don't reckon I'd fancy fried soup.
                       Too salty.

WOMAN I   My gawd!

MRS HICKERY   I wish that ~~b-blessed~~ Flaming bus would come. These
                       chips will be stone cold by the time I get home.

WOMAN II   (looking hungrily at the chips) Funny, that's
                       just what I was thinking.

                       (Enter MRS FINNEY SL, obviously hurrying for
                       the bus. She drops one of her shopping bags,
                       causing the contents to scatter all over the place.
                       She wilts like a broken reed, very out of breath.)

MRS FINNEY   Oooh, thought I'd missed it.... oh.... rushing
                       fit to burst a blood-vessel, I've been ... Ooooh!

(as she surveys the scattered contents of her bag) Oh, now look what I've done!

MRS HICKERY   (trying to take her arm and sit her down) Sit down, for goodness' sake, ~~Mrs Finney.~~ Sit down and calm down. The way you're rushing around you'll h~~ave one of your turns~~ again! *Drop your sprog*

Mrs Finney – TINA

TINA IS PREGNANT

(MRS FINNEY sits down on same bench as the rest of them. MRS HICKERY and WOMAN II collect the scattered contents.)

~~MRS FINNEY~~   Oooh .... thought I'd never make it .... oooh,
TINA   glad I got here in time... Ooh! Oh dear, oh
                dear~~!~~ *God!* *God*

MRS HICKERY   (to WOMAN II) Oh dear, oh dear is right. Always dashing around like a two-year old, she is. She'll do it once too often one of these days.

MRS FINNEY   Met Mrs What's-'er-name in Woolworth's and you know how she talks. Talk, talk, talk. Couldn't get away from her. One long moan, of course.

WOMAN I   I know that sort - one long moan!

MRS HICKERY   (handing bag with contents back to MRS FINNEY) There you are, Mrs Finney. *TINA* Are you feeling more yourself now, dear? (sits next to her) *Long Beach*
                love

MRS FINNEY   Not so bad, love, not so bad. Just in time, am I?

WOMAN I   In time for what?

MRS FINNEY   The bus, of course. Oh, wish I had a drop of brandy.

WOMAN I   Don't we all!

MRS HICKERY   How's y~~our Wil~~lie these days? Haven't seen him *DAVE* around lately.

MRS FINNEY   He's joined the police force - let me see - must be over twelve months now.

MRS HICKERY   Oh well, gives him something to do, I suppose.

MRS FINNEY   Looks ever so nice in his uniform, he does. He was a bit on the short side at first - had to take stretching exercises.

MRS HICKERY	Stretching exercises? What kind of stretching exercises?
MRS FINNEY	Oh, quite easy ones. The best one was hanging by his hands from the kitchen door.
WOMAN I	(drily) Sounds fun!
MRS FINNEY	Oh, he didn't laugh much when he was doing it. And it played havoc with the paint.

**(From SR a COUPLE make their entrance, arms around each other, almost literally wrapped around one another. They are, needless to say, completely oblivious to everyone and everything else. They make a snail's pace progress across the stage, stopping now and again to gaze into one another's eyes then finally exit SL. During their stage progress the following conversation takes place among the WOMEN, who, of course, are agog at the sight.
NB Care must be taken during this scene that when any of the WOMEN are speaking the COUPLE do not screen them from the audience.)

WOMAN I	(spotting the COUPLE as they enter) Hello, hello, hello – what have we here – (sniffs sarcastically) as if we didn't know!
WOMAN II	(with a soulful sigh) It's Love!
WOMAN I	Here we go again!
MRS HICKERY	All I can say is, the sooner they get married, the better.
WOMAN II	Well, they're only young once.
MRS HICKERY	What's that supposed to mean?
WOMAN II	Well – I mean – when you're young and all that – you know. I mean – well – you're YOUNG, aren't you? And – er – you're only young once.
WOMAN I	When you carry on like that, I reckon once is one time too many.
MRS HICKERY	They don't look that young, anyroad.
WOMAN II	Well .... you haven't GOT to be young, have you to – er – you know what I mean.

WOMAN I	(giving her an oldfashioned look) I thought you said your husband called you Modesty Mabel!
WOMAN II	(glancing aroung nervously) Sssh!
WOMAN I	What d'you mean - sssh?
WOMAN II	I told you confidential, like. Don't want everybody to know.
WOMAN I	Okay, okay. My lips are solid!
	(The COUPLE must have gone off SL by this point.)**
MRS HICKERY	(to MRS FINNEY) Shall we go and sit on that other bench? It's - er - warmer in the sun.
MRS FINNEY	Don't mind if I do.
	(They gather up all their bits and pieces and go to the other bench SR, watched in disapproving silence by WOMAN I and in innocent surprise by WOMAN II.)
MRS HICKERY	(settling herself) Funny woman.
MRS FINNEY	Yes. Which one?
MRS HICKERY	The one with her hat on back to front.
MRS FINNEY	(looking) Oh, yes, so it is.
MRS HICKERY	Lovely husband she's got.
MRS FINNEY	Has she, now?
MRS HICKERY	Get's a dog's life, of course. Nag, nag, nag.
MRS FINNEY	Always the same, I reckon. The good uns get the bad uns and vera vicey.
MRS HICKERY	You said it. Nag, like I said. I can always tell a nagger a mile off.
MRS FINNEY	Oh ... how?
MRS HICKERY	It's their mouths, girl. You look at their mouths. Look at her's, now.... go on ... she's not looking at us.
MRS FINNEY	I reckon she's got a moustache coming.
MRS HICKERY	Never mind her moustache. Look at her lips -

the way they turn down. Nearly touching her ...
well, you can see for yourself, can't you?

MRS FINNEY   That's right. They are, too.

WOMAN I   (belligerently) What you staring at me for? I
                got a spot on my nose or something?

MRS FINNEY   (confused) No, no – certainly not. I – we – er
                (suddenly inspired) – It's your hat. I were
                thinking what a lovely 'at it is.

WOMAN I   (appeased) Oh – me 'at. (touches it proudly)
                Got it in a sale I did. British Homes. The girl
                in the shop said it did something for me.

MRS HICKERY   (sotto voce) She was right, too!

WOMAN I   What's that you said?

MRS HICKERY   I wasn't speaking to you. I were speaking to my
                friend here.

MRS FINNEY   (pointing at audience) Oh, look, ~~Mrs Hickery~~ Angela –
                in that car there. There's Liza Brick!

MRS HICKERY   Where?

MRS FINNEY   That green car. They've had to slow down because
                of the traffic. (she waves, calling out:) ~~Coo-ee!~~ Oorey...

MRS HICKERY   So it is. (in a tone of scandalised delight) Oooh,
                did you see who she was with?

MRS FINNEY   Her husband, wasn't it?

MRS HICKERY   Don't make me laugh! She's a widow. It's (she
                whispers in MRS FINNEY's ear)

MRS FINNEY   No! Never!

MRS HICKERY   'S'fact! Over six months now.

MRS FINNEY   Well, well. And me thinking she was such a tidy
                little woman.

WOMAN I   (loudly) She IS a tidy little woman.

                (MRS HICKERY and MRS FINNEY are slightly
                shaken by this sudden onslaught.)

MRS HICKERY   (mustering a little dignity) I beg yer pardon?

WOMAN I   I said – Liza Brick is a tidy little woman. That

	was her husband driving the car. She's got married again.
MRS HICKERY	Oh! I wish I'd known. I'd 'ave sent her a present.
WOMAN I	Married to my second cousin's brother-in-law she is.
MRS HICKERY	Fancy!
WOMAN I	Not fancy - fact. So you be careful what you say.
MRS HICKERY	(regaining confidence fast) Are you incinerating something?
WOMAN I	I'm not incinerating anything. All I'm saying is just you be careful, that's all.
WOMAN II	(nervously trying to change the subject) Those chips do smell lovely.
MRS HICKERY	Yes, they do, don't they? I might as well eat them now, I reckon. They're going to be stone cold before that blasted bus comes.
	(Watched hungrily by the other three, she opens the paper, taking off layer after layer, then she begins to eat them with relish.)
	(critically) Could do with a bit more salt.
WOMAN II	(licking her lips) I likes plenty of salt, too.
MRS HICKERY	(offering bag to MRS FINNEY) Like a couple?
MRS FINNEY	Ta. (takes one then another and another) Nicest chips I've tasted for a long time.
MRS HICKERY	Not bad.
WOMAN II	I could tell by the smell that they'd be nice.
MRS FINNEY	Always tastes nicer out of the paper.
WOMAN II	That's what Bert - he's my husband - always says. Always tastes nicer straight out of the paper, he says.
	(WOMAN I, who has been keeping a frozen silence, delves into her bag and finds her half eaten banana in the brown paper bag and proceeds to eat it.)
	Oh! I forgot to get bananas!

WOMAN I	Tough luck!
WOMAN II	(plaintively) I'm always forgetting something.
WOMAN I	Eat a banana every day, I do. Good for the blood.
WOMAN II	(astonished) Good for the blood! Well, I never knew that.
MRS HICKERY	(rolling up chip paper into a ball and putting it down on the seat beside her) That's that. Feel a bit better now, I do.

S.R

(Two well-dressed women, ANITA and FIONA, enter SL. They look at the two benches and their occupants as though mentally debating where to sit. ANITA sees the rolled up ball of paper and, first removing her glove, picks it up with two distasteful fingers and drops it into the litter bin on the bus stop sign. As the bin has no bottom the paper, of course, falls to the ground. Needless to say, they have been watched with avid interest by the other four women.)

FIONA	(as paper falls) That's the Council for you, darling.
ANITA	And they ask you to keep Britain tidy!

(ANITA stands looking helplessly at the paper as if expecting it to leap into the bin of its own accord. WOMAN I gets up from her bench, picks up the paper and fixes it firmly on the rim of the bin and then sits down again.)

FIONA	We might as well sit down, I suppose.

(They move to the SC bench causing WOMAN I and WOMAN II to move their shopping bags with a great deal of fuss.)

ANITA	Do you know, I really cannot recall the last time I travelled by bus. Can you, Fiona?
FIONA	Now .... let me think .....
WOMAN I	(nudging WOMAN II violently) Wish I couldn't remember.
WOMAN II	(embarrassed) Sssssh!

FIONA	It must have been the last time Jeremy's car was being serviced - before I had my Rover.
WOMAN I	We had a dog called Rover.
WOMAN II	Fancy!
WOMAN I	And what d'you think he went and did?
WOMAN II	I dunno. What?
WOMAN I	He went and had pups.
WOMAN II	(dead serious) Fancy! Very confusing, that. But we all make mistakes, don't we?
ANITA	Such a nuisance - being without a car. I feel positively bereft.
FIONA	I do so agree, Anita darling. Almost a NAKED feeling. So EXPOSED - if you know what I mean.
	(Significant looks are exchanged by the others on hearing such basic sentiments.)
ANITA	Oh, I do, my dear, I do.
FIONA	By the by, how is Maxwell getting on since he came down from Oxford? He's in the City, isn't he?
ANITA	Well, he was, my dear, but actually he's left the City now.
FIONA	Really? Didn't he like it?
ANITA	It wasn't a question of LIKING it, Fiona. It was the PACE.
FIONA	The pace, my dear? What do you mean?
ANITA	He had to be in the office by ten thirty every morning - every single day - and work until half-past three.
FIONA	Oh, my dear! I do sympathise. Utter, utter slavery.
ANITA	And only two hours off for lunch.
FIONA	Only two hours! Positively brutal!
ANITA	I do wish that wretched bus would come. I have a luncheon engagement.
FIONA	(to others) Do you have any idea when the bus

	will be here?
WOMAN I	(poker face) What bus?
FIONA	This is a bus stop, isn't it?
WOMAN I	Who says?
FIONA	Who says! There! (points to bus stop sign) It says Bus Stop.
WOMAN I	Oh, that! You don't have to take any notice of that.
FIONA	Really?
ANITA	Why ever not?
WOMAN I	Left over from the last war, that is.
ANITA	The last war? Are you sure?
WOMAN I	True as I'm sitting here. Put up to mislead the Germans.
FIONA	Mislead the Germans?
WOMAN I	That's right.
ANITA	Oh, they did do that, didn't they? I seem to remember.
FIONA	Did they, really! Before my time, I'm afraid.
ANITA	Well, if this isn't a bus stop, what are you waiting for?
WOMAN I	That's my business, isn't it?
FIONA	It isn't the start of a demonstration for something, is it?
	(The others look at each other. WOMAN II looks startled.)
WOMAN II	Demonstration! Me? Oh, no.
WOMAN I	Maybe you're not, but what about us?
ANITA	(looking from one to the other appraisingly) I see. (to WOMAN II) So you are waiting for a bus?
WOMAN II	Oh, yes. Definitely.
ANITA	Good! We are in the right place, Fiona.

handwritten annotation: I don't remember being told that

WOMAN I   (to WOMAN II) Blackleg!

                    (There is the sound of a car horn tooting away.)

ANITA   (looking out at audience) Oh, look, there's
                    Charles just going round the corner. He's been
                    to get the car. Come on, we'll give you a lift.

FIONA   Oh, super!   S.L.

ANITA   (as they hurry SR) What a narrow escape!

FIONA   Escape, darling?

ANITA   From having to travel by bus. Hurry!

                    (They make good their escape off R.) (Left)

WOMAN I   Wish I could have a narrow escape.

MRS HICKERY   Some folks get all the luck.

WOMAN II   (wistfully) Nice name – Charles.

WOMAN I   (indifferently) You reckon!

MRS FINNEY   My old man's name is Charles. (take Micky)
                    old man's name is

WOMAN II   Fancy!

MRS FINNEY   Never 'eard him called that, mind. Always
                    Charlie.

WOMAN II   Fancy!

MRS FINNEY   There's times he is a right Charlie, too.

WOMAN I   We all got our troubles.

MRS FINNEY   Oh, I wouldn't call him trouble – not really. Gets
                    on my pip sometimes, of course.
                         nerves

MRS HICKERY   I reckon they all do.

WOMAN II   (innocently) Who?

MRS HICKERY   Men!

WOMAN I   Did you see her fur coat?

WOMAN II   Whose fur coat?

WOMAN I   Her, the one who spoke all posh like they do on the
                    BBC, Fiona. (exaggerate – Fee-yo-na)

MRS HICKERY   I saw it all right. That never came off the back of
                    a rabbit.

MRS FINNEY	Mink, I reckon.
WOMAN II	(proudly) I got a fur coat.
WOMAN I	(regarding her sceptically) Oh, yeh? Mink?
WOMAN II	Pardon?
WOMAN I	I asked if it were mink?
WOMAN II	I ain't quite sure, really.
WOMAN I	One of them mystery fur coats, is it?
WOMAN II	(innocently) I don't know that sort.
WOMAN I	They got them in Tesco's.
WOMAN II	Oh, I never got mine from Tesco's.
WOMAN I	Oh? Where, then?
WOMAN II	Don't know, really. It was my husband, see – Bert. He came home one night and said to me – Ingrid, he said –
WOMAN I	(surprised for once) Ingrid?
WOMAN II	That's me name – Ingrid. Ingrid, he said, I got a lovely surprise for you. And there it was – my lovely fur coat.
WOMAN I	It didn't fall off the back of a lorry, did it?
WOMAN II	Oh, no. It was all nice and clean. (in sudden recollection) Oh!
WOMAN I	What's the matter?
WOMAN II	I just remembered what kind it is. Bert told me. It's genuine stimulated fur.
MRS HICKERY	That's the best kind, I reckon – genuine <u>simulated</u>.
MRS FINNEY	My first husband – no, I'm telling a lie – it was my second – he was in the fur trade.
WOMAN I	What did he do? Skin rabbits?
MRS FINNEY	You trying to take the mickey?
WOMAN I	Me? Whatever for? I'm not Irish.
WOMAN II	(to the rescue) Oh, dear, I do wish the bus would come. I feel sinking.

WOMAN I   Did you say - stinking?

WOMAN II   (protesting) No - sinking. I baths regular every Friday night.

(The BOOKWORM enters SR, her head buried in a tome of a book and a shoulder bag swinging carelessly over one shoulder.)

WOMAN I   (again the first to notice the newcomer) Hello, hello! What have we here?

WOMAN II   She's reading.

WOMAN I   I didn't think she was doing the splits.

(Every couple of steps the BOOKWORM stops and turns over a page.)

Damn quick reader.

MRS HICKERY   I'm a big reader myself. Red Letter and Woman - every week.

MRS FINNEY   You're lucky. I haven't got time to read. What with the washing and the ironing and the shopping and the cooking and the kids and the -

WOMAN I   (interposing neatly) - we got all that.

(The BOOKWORM's shoulder bag slipped to the ground unnoticed during the last speech and she is now a few feet away from it SL.)

WOMAN II   Oh, she's dropped her bag.

WOMAN I   Better bring her back to earth, I suppose.

(WOMAN I gets up, picks up the bag and taps the BOOKWORM on the shoulder. She looks up vaguely.)

BOOKWORM   How d'you do?

WOMAN I   (automatically) Quite well, thank you.

BOOKWORM   (continuing on her way) So glad to hear it. Good morning.

WOMAN I   Wait a minute, professor. You dropped this.

BOOKWORM   (peers at bag short-sightedly) This?

WOMAN I   Your bag, ducky, your bag.

BOOKWORM   Are you sure? (looks at her shoulder - still in a

	dream) It was there - I'm sure it was.
WOMAN I	I know. But it fell off.
BOOKWORM	Oh ... oh. I see! Thank you ... thank you ... (taking bag) So kind.
WOMAN I	(returning to bench) Some mothers do 'ave 'em!
BOOKWORM	(having taken a couple of steps SL then stopped and turned back abruptly) Er, excuse me.....?
WOMAN I	Yes?
BOOKWORM	I hesitate to -er- intrude - but are you by any chance waiting for a bus?
ALL FOUR	(together) YES!
BOOKWORM	Oh dear!
WOMAN I	What d'you mean - oh dear?
BOOKWORM	You haven't heard the news, have you?
WOMAN I	What are you on about?
MRS HICKERY	What news?
BOOKWORM	They call it industrial action.
WOMAN II	Industrial action?
BOOKWORM	Actually it means inaction. The bus people - they've gone on strike.
	(She returns to her book and exits SL reading. The four WOMEN are stunned then annoyed.)
ALL FOUR	Bus strike!.... After waiting all this time ...... Good job I ate my chips .... Don't know what things are coming to .... It's a disgrace .... Wish my old man would come past in a flashy car.. .... Typical of our flippin' public services ..... (ad lib)
	(They collect their bags and move wearily SL muttering and grumbling, MRS HICKERY and MRS FINNEY in the lead.)
WOMAN I	(from the back of the line) You wait till I get home ..... I'll give him industrial action!
WOMAN II	What d'you want to go for your husband for? He

BUS STOP

can't help it, can he?

WOMAN I   (angrily) Can't he ... can't he? He works on
the b-blessed buses!

BLACKOUT

CURTAIN

29 mins